EMMANUEL JOSEPH

Harmonious Synergies, Navigating the Intersection of Growth, Prosperity, and Connection

Copyright © 2025 by Emmanuel Joseph

All rights reserved. No part of this publication may be reproduced, stored or transmitted in any form or by any means, electronic, mechanical, photocopying, recording, scanning, or otherwise without written permission from the publisher. It is illegal to copy this book, post it to a website, or distribute it by any other means without permission.

First edition

This book was professionally typeset on Reedsy. Find out more at reedsy.com

Contents

1	Chapter 1: The Foundations of Growth	1
2	Chapter 2: Defining Prosperity in Modern Times	3
3	Chapter 3: The Synergy of Growth and Prosperity	5
4	Chapter 4: Navigating the Challenges of Modern Life	7
5	Chapter 5: Cultivating Meaningful Relationships	9
6	Chapter 6: The Power of Community and Collaboration	11
7	Chapter 7: Embracing Diversity and Inclusion	13
8	Chapter 8: The Intersection of Technology and Human...	15
9	Chapter 9: Mindfulness and Presence in Daily Life	16
10	Chapter 10: The Role of Purpose and Passion	18
11	Chapter 11: Balancing Ambition and Well-being	20
12	Chapter 12: The Art of Adaptability	22
13	Chapter 13: Financial Literacy and Empowerment	23
14	Chapter 14: The Future of Growth and Prosperity	25
15	Chapter 15: Conclusion - Creating a Harmonious and...	27

1

Chapter 1: The Foundations of Growth

Growth is an inherent aspect of life, whether it's personal, professional, or societal. It starts with the realization that change is not just inevitable but necessary for progress. Embracing growth requires an open mind, a willingness to learn, and the courage to step out of one's comfort zone. This chapter explores the psychological and emotional foundations of growth, delving into the importance of mindset, resilience, and adaptability.

In understanding growth, it's crucial to recognize the role of failure and setbacks. These experiences, while often painful, serve as valuable lessons that shape our future endeavors. By reframing failures as opportunities for learning and growth, we can cultivate a more resilient and proactive approach to challenges. This chapter also examines the role of mentorship and support systems in fostering personal and professional development.

Furthermore, growth is not a solitary journey but one that involves collaboration and connection. Building strong relationships with others can provide the support and encouragement needed to overcome obstacles and achieve our goals. This chapter highlights the importance of networking, teamwork, and communication in fostering growth in various aspects of life.

Finally, the chapter addresses the concept of sustainable growth. It emphasizes the need to balance ambition with mindfulness, ensuring that our pursuits do not come at the expense of our well-being or the environment.

By adopting sustainable practices and prioritizing self-care, we can create a more harmonious and fulfilling path to growth.

2

Chapter 2: Defining Prosperity in Modern Times

Prosperity is often equated with wealth and material success, but its true essence encompasses much more. In this chapter, we redefine prosperity to include not only financial stability but also emotional well-being, meaningful relationships, and a sense of purpose. This holistic approach recognizes that true prosperity is multidimensional, touching all aspects of our lives.

Economic prosperity is undoubtedly a significant component, but it's essential to understand its limitations. The pursuit of wealth, while important, should not overshadow other facets of life that contribute to our overall happiness and fulfillment. This chapter delves into the balance between financial success and personal satisfaction, exploring the concept of work-life integration.

Emotional and mental well-being are critical to experiencing true prosperity. This chapter discusses the importance of mental health, self-awareness, and emotional intelligence in achieving a prosperous life. By cultivating mindfulness and self-compassion, we can better navigate the complexities of modern living and build a foundation for lasting happiness.

Furthermore, prosperity extends to our relationships and sense of community. Building and maintaining meaningful connections with others enriches our lives and provides a support system during challenging times. This chapter explores the role of empathy, communication, and collaboration in fostering a prosperous and connected society.

3

Chapter 3: The Synergy of Growth and Prosperity

Growth and prosperity are often viewed as separate pursuits, but they are intrinsically linked. This chapter explores the dynamic interplay between these two concepts, highlighting how one can fuel and enhance the other. By understanding and leveraging this synergy, we can create a more holistic and fulfilling path to success.

Personal and professional growth often lead to increased opportunities and, consequently, greater prosperity. This chapter examines the ways in which continuous learning, skill development, and adaptability contribute to financial stability and success. It also discusses the importance of setting clear goals and maintaining a growth-oriented mindset to achieve long-term prosperity.

Conversely, achieving prosperity can provide the resources and stability needed to pursue further growth. Financial security allows us to invest in our education, personal development, and well-being, creating a positive feedback loop that enhances both growth and prosperity. This chapter delves into the importance of financial planning and resource management in supporting sustainable growth.

Moreover, the synergy between growth and prosperity extends to our relationships and communities. By fostering a culture of collaboration and mutual support, we can create environments where individuals and groups can thrive. This chapter explores the role of social networks, mentorship, and community engagement in promoting a harmonious balance between growth and prosperity.

4

Chapter 4: Navigating the Challenges of Modern Life

In today's fast-paced and ever-changing world, navigating the challenges of modern life requires resilience, adaptability, and a proactive mindset. This chapter delves into the various obstacles we face in our personal and professional lives and offers strategies for overcoming them. By understanding and addressing these challenges, we can create a more harmonious and fulfilling existence.

One of the most significant challenges in modern life is the constant pressure to succeed and meet societal expectations. This chapter explores the impact of stress, burnout, and imposter syndrome on our well-being and offers practical tips for managing these pressures. By prioritizing self-care and setting realistic goals, we can maintain a healthier balance and avoid the pitfalls of overachievement.

Technological advancements have brought numerous benefits but also present unique challenges. This chapter discusses the impact of digital overload, information fatigue, and the erosion of work-life boundaries on our mental health and relationships. It offers strategies for managing technology use, setting boundaries, and maintaining meaningful connections in the digital age.

Furthermore, modern life is characterized by increasing complexity and uncertainty. This chapter examines the importance of adaptability and resilience in navigating these challenges. It discusses the role of mindset, problem-solving skills, and emotional intelligence in overcoming obstacles and thriving in an unpredictable world.

5

Chapter 5: Cultivating Meaningful Relationships

Meaningful relationships are the cornerstone of a fulfilling and prosperous life. This chapter explores the importance of building and maintaining strong connections with others, both personally and professionally. By fostering empathy, communication, and trust, we can create a supportive network that enhances our growth and well-being.

Building meaningful relationships starts with self-awareness and emotional intelligence. This chapter discusses the importance of understanding our own needs, boundaries, and communication styles to form authentic connections with others. It also highlights the role of active listening, empathy, and vulnerability in creating deeper and more meaningful interactions.

Maintaining strong relationships requires ongoing effort and commitment. This chapter delves into the importance of nurturing and sustaining connections through regular communication, shared experiences, and mutual support. It offers practical tips for maintaining healthy relationships and resolving conflicts constructively.

Moreover, meaningful relationships extend beyond personal connections to our professional and community networks. This chapter explores the role of networking, collaboration, and community engagement in building a prosperous and connected society. By fostering a culture of support and cooperation, we can create environments where individuals and groups can thrive together.

6

Chapter 6: The Power of Community and Collaboration

Communities play a vital role in shaping our lives and experiences. This chapter examines the power of community and collaboration in fostering growth, prosperity, and connection. By building strong, supportive communities, we can create environments where individuals and groups can thrive and achieve their full potential.

The foundation of a strong community lies in shared values, goals, and a sense of belonging. This chapter discusses the importance of fostering inclusivity, diversity, and mutual respect within our communities. It explores the role of empathy, communication, and collaboration in creating a supportive and cohesive environment.

Collaboration is a key component of successful communities. This chapter delves into the benefits of working together, sharing resources, and pooling talents to achieve common goals. It offers practical tips for fostering a collaborative mindset and building effective partnerships within personal, professional, and community contexts.

Moreover, communities provide a support system that can help individuals navigate challenges and achieve their goals. This chapter examines the role of mentorship, peer support, and community engagement in fostering personal and collective growth. By building strong networks and nurturing a culture of support, we can create resilient and thriving communities.

7

Chapter 7: Embracing Diversity and Inclusion

Diversity and inclusion are essential for creating vibrant, innovative, and prosperous communities. This chapter explores the importance of embracing diversity in all its forms and fostering an inclusive environment where everyone can thrive. By valuing and celebrating differences, we can unlock the full potential of our communities and achieve greater growth and prosperity.

Understanding the benefits of diversity is the first step toward creating inclusive communities. This chapter discusses the positive impact of diverse perspectives, experiences, and backgrounds on problem-solving, creativity, and innovation. It highlights the importance of fostering an open and respectful dialogue to ensure that all voices are heard and valued.

Creating an inclusive environment requires intentional effort and commitment. This chapter delves into the strategies for promoting inclusivity, such as implementing equitable policies, providing education and training, and actively addressing biases and discrimination. It offers practical tips for building a culture of inclusion within personal, professional, and community contexts.

Moreover, embracing diversity and inclusion extends beyond individual actions to systemic change. This chapter examines the role of leadership, advocacy, and collective action in promoting social justice and equity. By working together to dismantle barriers and create opportunities for all, we can build a more inclusive and prosperous society.

8

Chapter 8: The Intersection of Technology and Human Connection

Technology has transformed the way we live, work, and connect with others. This chapter explores the intersection of technology and human connection, examining both the opportunities and challenges that arise in the digital age. By leveraging technology responsibly and mindfully, we can enhance our connections and create a more harmonious and connected world.

The rise of digital communication tools has revolutionized the way we interact with others. This chapter discusses the benefits of technology in fostering connections, such as facilitating communication, expanding networks, and bridging geographical distances. It also highlights the role of social media and online communities in creating a sense of belonging and shared purpose.

However, the digital age also presents unique challenges to human connection. This chapter delves into the impact of digital overload, information fatigue, and the erosion of face-to-face interactions on our relationships and well-being. It offers strategies for managing technology use, setting boundaries, and maintaining meaningful connections in the digital age.

9

Chapter 9: Mindfulness and Presence in Daily Life

Mindfulness and presence are powerful practices that can enhance our overall well-being and connections with others. This chapter explores the importance of being present in the moment and cultivating mindfulness in our daily lives. By developing these practices, we can create a more harmonious and fulfilling existence.

Mindfulness involves paying attention to our thoughts, emotions, and sensations without judgment. This chapter discusses the benefits of mindfulness, such as reducing stress, enhancing focus, and improving emotional regulation. It offers practical tips for incorporating mindfulness into daily routines, such as meditation, deep breathing exercises, and mindful eating.

Being present in our interactions with others is crucial for building meaningful relationships. This chapter delves into the importance of active listening, empathy, and non-verbal communication in creating genuine connections. It highlights the role of presence in fostering trust, understanding, and mutual respect in our personal and professional relationships.

Moreover, mindfulness and presence can enhance our productivity and decision-making. This chapter examines the impact of mindfulness on cognitive function, creativity, and problem-solving skills. By cultivating a mindful approach to work and daily tasks, we can improve our efficiency

CHAPTER 9: MINDFULNESS AND PRESENCE IN DAILY LIFE

and achieve a greater sense of accomplishment.

10

Chapter 10: The Role of Purpose and Passion

Finding and pursuing our purpose and passion is essential for leading a fulfilling and prosperous life. This chapter explores the importance of identifying our core values, interests, and strengths to create a sense of purpose and direction. By aligning our actions with our passions, we can achieve greater satisfaction and meaning in our lives.

Purpose provides a sense of direction and motivation, guiding our choices and actions. This chapter discusses the benefits of having a clear sense of purpose, such as increased resilience, improved mental health, and enhanced well-being. It offers practical tips for discovering and clarifying our purpose, such as self-reflection, goal-setting, and seeking feedback from others.

Pursuing our passions involves aligning our interests and strengths with our daily activities and long-term goals. This chapter delves into the importance of passion in driving motivation, creativity, and persistence. It highlights the role of passion in achieving personal and professional success and offers strategies for integrating our passions into our lives.

Moreover, purpose and passion extend beyond individual pursuits to creating a positive impact on others and the world. This chapter examines the role of purpose-driven work, volunteerism, and social impact in fostering a sense of fulfillment and connection. By aligning our actions with our

CHAPTER 10: THE ROLE OF PURPOSE AND PASSION

values and passions, we can contribute to a more prosperous and harmonious society.

11

Chapter 11: Balancing Ambition and Well-being

Balancing ambition and well-being is essential for achieving long-term success and happiness. This chapter explores the importance of setting ambitious goals while prioritizing self-care and mental health. By finding a harmonious balance, we can achieve our aspirations without compromising our well-being.

Ambition drives us to set challenging goals and strive for excellence. This chapter discusses the benefits of ambition, such as increased motivation, resilience, and personal growth. It offers practical tips for setting realistic and achievable goals, maintaining a growth mindset, and staying focused on our aspirations.

However, excessive ambition can lead to burnout, stress, and a decline in well-being. This chapter delves into the importance of self-care, mindfulness, and work-life balance in maintaining our mental and emotional health. It highlights the role of self-awareness and self-compassion in recognizing our limits and prioritizing our well-being.

Moreover, balancing ambition and well-being requires a holistic approach to success. This chapter examines the importance of integrating various aspects of our lives, such as career, relationships, health, and personal growth, to achieve a fulfilling and prosperous life. By adopting a balanced and mindful

CHAPTER 11: BALANCING AMBITION AND WELL-BEING

approach to our ambitions, we can create a more harmonious and sustainable path to success.

12

Chapter 12: The Art of Adaptability

Adaptability is a crucial skill for navigating the complexities and uncertainties of modern life. This chapter explores the importance of being flexible and open to change, both personally and professionally. By cultivating adaptability, we can thrive in an ever-changing world and achieve greater growth and prosperity.

Adaptability involves being open to new experiences, ideas, and perspectives. This chapter discusses the benefits of adaptability, such as increased resilience, problem-solving skills, and creativity. It offers practical tips for developing adaptability, such as embracing change, seeking feedback, and learning from diverse experiences.

In the professional realm, adaptability is essential for staying relevant and competitive. This chapter delves into the importance of continuous learning, skill development, and innovation in the workplace. It highlights the role of adaptability in career growth and success, offering strategies for navigating industry changes and technological advancements.

Moreover, adaptability extends to our personal lives and relationships. This chapter examines the importance of being flexible and responsive in our interactions with others. It discusses the role of empathy, communication, and conflict resolution in maintaining harmonious and supportive relationships. By cultivating adaptability, we can create a more resilient and connected life.

13

Chapter 13: Financial Literacy and Empowerment

Financial literacy and empowerment are essential for achieving long-term prosperity and security. This chapter explores the importance of understanding and managing our finances, making informed decisions, and building financial resilience. By developing financial literacy, we can create a more stable and prosperous future.

Financial literacy involves understanding basic financial concepts, such as budgeting, saving, investing, and debt management. This chapter discusses the benefits of financial literacy, such as increased financial security, reduced stress, and improved decision-making. It offers practical tips for developing financial literacy, such as seeking education, setting financial goals, and creating a budget.

Empowerment involves taking control of our financial future and making informed decisions. This chapter delves into the importance of financial planning, risk management, and goal-setting in achieving financial empowerment. It highlights the role of financial advisors, tools, and resources in supporting our financial journey.

Moreover, financial literacy and empowerment extend beyond individual prosperity to creating a positive impact on others and our communities. This chapter examines the importance of financial education, philanthropy, and social responsibility in fostering a more equitable and prosperous society. By sharing our knowledge and resources, we can contribute to a more financially empowered world.

14

Chapter 14: The Future of Growth and Prosperity

As we look to the future, the concepts of growth and prosperity will continue to evolve and shape our lives. This chapter explores emerging trends and challenges that will impact our pursuit of growth and prosperity in the coming years. By staying informed and adaptable, we can navigate these changes and create a more harmonious and prosperous future.

Technological advancements, such as artificial intelligence, automation, and digital transformation, will play a significant role in shaping the future of work and society. This chapter discusses the potential benefits and challenges of these technologies, such as increased efficiency, job displacement, and ethical considerations. It offers strategies for staying relevant and adaptable in a rapidly changing world.

Environmental sustainability and social responsibility will also be critical factors in the future of growth and prosperity. This chapter delves into the importance of adopting sustainable practices, promoting social equity, and addressing global challenges, such as climate change and resource depletion. It highlights the role of innovation, collaboration, and collective action in creating a more sustainable and prosperous future.

Moreover, the future of growth and prosperity will be influenced by changing demographics, cultural shifts, and global interconnectedness. This chapter examines the impact of these trends on our personal and professional lives, exploring the opportunities and challenges they present. By embracing diversity, fostering inclusivity, and staying open to change, we can create a more harmonious and connected world.

15

Chapter 15: Conclusion - Creating a Harmonious and Prosperous Life

In conclusion, achieving growth, prosperity, and connection requires a holistic and mindful approach to life. This chapter summarizes the key concepts and strategies discussed throughout the book and offers practical steps for creating a harmonious and prosperous future.

Growth involves continuous learning, adaptability, and resilience. By embracing change and seeking new experiences, we can achieve personal and professional development. Prosperity extends beyond financial success to include emotional well-being, meaningful relationships, and a sense of purpose. By prioritizing self-care, fostering connections, and aligning our actions with our values, we can achieve a fulfilling and prosperous life.

Connection is the foundation of a harmonious and supportive society. Building and maintaining meaningful relationships, fostering collaboration, and embracing diversity are essential for creating a connected and thriving world. By working together and supporting one another, we can create environments where individuals and communities can flourish.

Ultimately, creating a harmonious and prosperous life involves balancing ambition with well-being, cultivating mindfulness and presence, and staying adaptable in the face of change. By adopting these practices and principles, we can navigate the intersection of growth, prosperity, and connection, creating a more fulfilling and meaningful life.

Description:

In an ever-evolving world, finding the balance between growth, prosperity, and meaningful connections can seem like a daunting task. "Harmonious Synergies" delves deep into the intricate dance of these three essential facets of life, offering readers a comprehensive guide to navigate their intersection.

From the psychological foundations of personal and professional growth to redefining prosperity in modern times, this book presents a holistic approach to achieving success and fulfillment. It underscores the importance of building strong, meaningful relationships and communities that support and uplift us.

Through 15 insightful chapters, readers will explore the synergy between growth and prosperity, the challenges of modern life, and the power of mindfulness and presence. The book also addresses the role of purpose and passion, the balance between ambition and well-being, and the art of adaptability in an ever-changing world.

"Harmonious Synergies" is not just a guide but a companion on the journey to a balanced and prosperous life. It emphasizes the importance of financial literacy, the future of growth and prosperity, and the impact of diversity, inclusion, and technology on our connections and well-being.

Whether you seek personal development, professional success, or stronger connections, this book offers practical strategies and profound insights to help you create a harmonious and fulfilling life. Discover the path to true prosperity and connection in a world where growth is not just possible but essential.

www.ingramcontent.com/pod-product-compliance
Lightning Source LLC
Chambersburg PA
CBHW072023290426
44109CB00018B/2325